SAVED NOT SINGLE

Redefining Singleness for the Believer

Emmanual Benton

Saved Not Single

Redefining Singleness for the Believer

by

Emmanual Benton

Copyright © 2023

ISBN: 979-8-218-23760-8

Harbens Publishing

First Edition

I was raised by a single mom who is a prayer warrior and loves God with her whole heart. I dedicate this book to her because I've watched her not allow relationships or the lack thereof to get in the way of raising me, but most importantly, serving the Lord. I know what contentment in the Lord looks like because of her.

I love you, Mom.

To my friends who are not yet married.
To my family who are not yet married.
To those who have grown up without much
theological footing on singleness.
I see you; I love you and I pray this book
serves you well.

For His glory!

Contents

Introduction

Writing this book was a way for me to exhale. It's not so much that being unmarried was suffocating me, there's just been so much that God has been showing me both about myself and the state of being unmarried, that I couldn't keep it to myself. I felt the Lord leading me to write a book that would serve somewhat as an apologetic for the way many view singleness for the believer. There is not a lack of resources on this subject, as there are many books, podcasts, and online content providing solid guidance for believers to live out their state of singleness well. However, I felt that sharing my story as an unmarried young black man in ministry would provide a unique vantage point.

My goal for this book was to offer a gospel-centered resource not only for unmarried believers, but also for those who *know* unmarried believers. It's not enough for unmarried believers to simply grow in understanding of how to navigate this state of life, it's also important for those who know them—whether friend, child, brother or sister—to learn how to speak into their life. I have learned one of the things that makes being unmarried most difficult is having to navigate what loved ones think or say about you being unmarried. Same for the Church, whether said or unsaid, there seems to be a hierarchy and married folk are atop that list. My desire is for *Saved, Not Single* to redefine the term singleness and to provide theology surrounding the subject. I wrote this book while in the state of being unmarried. Not only unmarried, but not even really dating.

Please note that the focus of this book is about singleness for the believer. It's about how to thrive as a Christian Single and how to view singleness within the faith. Lord willing, this book will be the first of a trilogy that will include "dating" and "married" titles.

This book is not to discourage the unmarried from getting married. I believe that the Lord has a call for every believer's life that isn't attached in marriage. In the book, I discuss how the gospel is for all people and that it not only saves but it sends. If I had to rest this book on one scripture, it would be Ephesians 2:8-10 (HSCB): "For you are saved by grace through faith, and this is not from yourselves; it is God's gift—not from works, so that no one can boast. For we are His creation, created in Christ Jesus for good works, which God prepared ahead of time so that we should walk in them."

Our relationship status does not define us. The fact that Jesus has saved us defines us. He saved us so that we may be sent out into a world that so desperately needs to hear about Him. I pray that this book draws the unmarried closer to Jesus and helps the married better serve the unmarried.

1

Relationship Status

For me, middle school was the time that pursuing a relationship became a real idea. If I'm being honest, it may have started a little before that in elementary school. But middle school is where I really began to feel the relationship pressure.

It almost felt like a necessity to have a girlfriend. Otherwise, you'd get labeled as being uncool, unattractive, or unwanted. You were identified by whether you were in a relationship or not. So I quickly succumbed to what appeared to be the cultural norm and began to believe that it was important to be in a relationship. At that point, dating wasn't even a term that existed. You would just ask a girl to be your girlfriend or to "go with you," whatever that even means.

Mid-way through my sixth grade year, I found out one of the more popular girls in my grade liked me. Of course, I was stoked. I remember leaving the cafeteria during lunchtime with a group of at least five friends to meet her in the hallway for a grand "proposal." She stood there also with a group of friends and I popped the question, "Will you go with me?" Her response was yes. So, all of a sudden I had my first girlfriend. It was a moment of my life that I'll never forget. Mostly because the relationship lasted less than 24 hours!

Later that night, I remember talking on the phone with the same friends who witnessed my proposal. They brought to light some concerns about this girl's reputation with boys in the past. You would think that would've been discussed prior to me making her my girlfriend. Nonetheless, I listened to my friends and ended the relationship that night on the phone. Although, we did remain "unofficially" an item for the remainder of the school year.

We texted and talked on the phone every single day. We attended basketball games together and exchanged Valentines with each other. We even reached the point where we would constantly exchange, "I love you," sentiments. Our relationship never reached dangerous territory, but I quickly realized it was unhealthy for me to continue entertaining her with no intent or direction.

So in seventh grade, I changed my approach. I decided that it was better for me not to emotionally invest so much into a girl. Yet, that necessity to have a girlfriend remained. That resulted in me essentially using girls as props. I used them to help sustain my cool kid status. The relationships didn't need to be defined. The attention and perception mattered most.

I found value in being able to get girls. It made me feel wanted, important and honestly like a man. I thought that's what it took to be considered those things. That way of thinking lasted until what I consider the turning point of my life.

Eighth grade is when I truly began to develop my personal relationship with God. I grew up in church, as my grandfather was a pastor. I always knew Jesus, but eighth grade is when I really surrendered everything to Him. I started to get involved at church by leading the worship team and serving as a youth ministry leader. I took those responsibilities seriously and it changed the trajectory of my life.

I remember when my grandfather initially offered me an opportunity to lead worship at church. Not only did he offer me the position, but he also sat me down and preached a whole sermon about the weight of the position. He taught me that worship is all about our response to our personal relationship with God. That really convicted my spirit about the way I was living my life. I knew God, but I didn't truly know Him for myself. As I started to build my personal relationship with the Lord, my heart's desires began to change. I started to discover my identity in Christ, putting away childish things and following Him wholeheartedly. 1 Corinthians 13:11, (NKJV) became very real to me, "When I was a child, I spoke like a child, I thought like a child, I reasoned as a child. When I became a man, I put aside childish things."

In that season of my life, the Lord had to do a work on my heart and strip away certain things. He convicted me a lot. Things like listening to secular music became something I had to put aside in that new season. I realized that listening to Hip Hop and R&B really began to affect my character.

Songs that glorified cheating, premarital sex and that "player mentality" polluted my mind. It is a tool the enemy can use to reach people at a young age. A lot of the songs I listened to had begun to paint a false picture of love and manhood. God really opened my eyes to these things, so I completely stopped listening to secular music for several years. It wasn't about being legalistic, it was about being more like Christ and being Spirit-led. My heart was convicted of all things that were not beneficial for me at that stage.

When you press into Jesus, everything changes. When He does a work on your heart, you begin to desire what He desires for you. Although I was still just a teenager, my manhood became tied to my relationship with Christ and not young women.

God began to sanctify me. I was no longer concerned about needing a girlfriend to be considered cool, important, wanted or a man. Bringing glory to God in every area of my life became most important. This doesn't mean I was perfect, because I absolutely was not, but God was and continues to perfect me. That should be the case in every Christian's life.

As I entered High School, I began to develop the mindset of not entering a relationship until I was ready to get married. I remember always telling myself that I wouldn't even begin to think about marriage until I was twenty-five years old. I don't know if that was the Holy Spirit or just a desire in my heart. I didn't necessarily have scripture as the foundation for those thoughts, but either way, I believe it was in accordance with what God desired for my young adult life. So I did just that. I refrained from dating.

I'll admit, there were numerous times in my high school and early young adult years that I developed feelings for a girl. Those feelings were superficial, but nonetheless, a challenge to navigate—God did not make me blind! Yet, every time I even considered approaching a beautiful young lady, the Lord would immediately reveal something negative about her character that would've conflicted with mine. He was telling me "no" each time. I even had several ladies that were bold enough to attempt initiating a relationship with me. But I was determined not to get into a relationship until I started to desire marriage.

I often think God blocked women that were worth pursuing, in terms of character, from my eyesight, even back in my high school and early young adult years. So honestly, dating wasn't even a realistic option for me. Even if I had come across someone worth pursuing at that stage in my life, not having a desire for marriage would have stopped me. There was no reason for me to date if marriage was not on my mind. Otherwise, I would be wasting both their time and mine. Not to mention, it would've opened the door to all kinds of temptation. When you place yourself in a dating situation that has no direction, you will be tempted to cross lines that shouldn't be crossed outside of marriage. It's bad enough that sexual temptation is already something that needs to be controlled *outside* of a relationship; *adding* a relationship will only intensify those challenges.

As I started to approach that twenty-five year mark, it's crazy, but I actually did begin to desire marriage. In fact, not merely did I desire marriage, but especially a godly relationship that would lead to a godly marriage. So I began to study and really prepare my heart. I remember finding a bunch of videos on YouTube and listening to podcasts, hoping to learn what a godly relationship looked like. Honestly, I didn't have much prior knowledge other than some of the wisdom God bestowed upon my heart. I also searched scripture to help develop my theology on dating, so that when I started dating, I'd be ready.

Unfortunately, I think God had other plans for me. In 2018, I turned twenty-five years old. The very next day my grandfather passed away. The day of my twenty-fifth birthday was the last time I saw my grandfather with breath in his lungs. Losing the most influential person in my life was not easy. He was more than a grandfather. He was like a father, closest friend, mentor, pastor, and so much more. His death changed a lot for me and the dynamic of my family. It also took me a while to reach a place where I felt healthy enough to date. I would say that it took me two years to really get back to that place where I was ready to pursue a relationship.

But then 2020 hit with a worldwide pandemic that shifted everyone's life. I really did not begin to start dipping my toe into the dating world until 2021 and here I am today, still unmarried! But I continue to have a strong desire for marriage. Therefore, unlike my pre-twenty-five-year-old self, I *do* feel a desire to date with a true purpose and goal in mind. The purpose or the reason is to find out if that person is your husband or wife, but the goal, which is your aim, is to glorify God. That goal should remain the same in every aspect of our lives. In all things, do it for the glory of God (1 Corinthians 10:31).

How Should This Goal and Purpose Compel the Unmarried?

I think it is unwise to pursue a relationship until your heart begins to desire marriage. I'm reluctant to say wait until you're ready, because I don't think you can ever be fully prepared for marriage. However, if you enter a relationship with the mindset of glorifying God, I am certain He will equip you for the tasks ahead.

You cannot glorify God in a dating relationship that is not intended to discover whether that person is your spouse. You absolutely cannot glorify God in a dating relationship that involves sex, as it goes against the Word of God. If you find yourself in one of those situations, I urge you to pump the breaks and turn to God. It may not be easy, but God forgives, strengthens, and guides, so trust that God can get you through it. This is why as Christians we must be careful and really evaluate our intentions when entering into a dating relationship.

Scripture doesn't speak of dating, courting (as some prefer it labeled) or even singleness for that matter. Scripture only speaks of the unmarried, married, divorced, and widowed. However, I find no issue with the terms dating, courting or singleness. The issue is that with dating or courting, if the relationship lacks that true purpose, it cannot glorify God.

Dating without purpose leads to things the Bible clearly considers sin. Sex outside marriage is sin (1 Corinthians 7:2). Dating can come with sexual temptations, especially if you are indeed attracted to that person. When you're in that relationship with the purpose of discovering if this person is your spouse and aiming towards glorifying God, He will give you strength to endure those temptations. However, a relationship with no purpose of discovering if this person is your spouse with no aim of glorifying God will likely lead you into fulfilling those sexual temptations. Why? Because if you're in a dating relationship with no purpose or goal, it's safe to believe that it is fueled merely by lust or an attempt to fill a void in your life. We are all subject to lust, but it is a sin that leads to more sin and we know that sin is a gateway to death (Romans 8:6). The Bible tells us to not allow lust to enter our hearts (Proverbs 6:25). Our hearts are deceitful (Jeremiah 17:9). This is why we must guard our hearts and depend on God for strength (Psalm 73:26). One way of guarding our hearts is to refrain from dating until you are ready to pursue marriage.

Identity In Christ

Dating is such a gray area. You're still unmarried, thus not bonded by covenant to a person. It's a time to gather information on each other. Dating is also a time to figure out if you are like-minded with that person, not merely in terms of attraction, but identity and purpose. Yet, if you have no identity and purpose, you could be wasting your time or setting yourself up for a challenging relationship. In this scenario, you have nothing to give. You have nothing to match. It is unlikely that God will be glorified in that situation.

In Genesis, before God decided to give Adam a wife, He gave Adam an identity. He gave Adam a purpose for life. It was Adam's responsibility to take care of the garden and to name all living things. Although this story can often be pigeonholed as a lesson only for men, I think this is also wisdom for women. We all should first discover our identity and purpose in Christ before ever stepping into a relationship; this glorifies God. In fact, before you can even love your neighbor, Jesus says you must first love the Lord your God with all your heart, soul and mind (Matthew 22:37). It is the first and greatest commandment.

I don't believe it's a stretch to say that Eve had both identity and purpose before she was even created. Remember, God first said it was not good for Adam to be alone. God didn't just create Eve and wonder what to do with her. She was created for a reason, thus having identity and purpose before Adam ever laid an eye on her. This is true for all of creation. We were created for a reason, but our God-ordained identity cannot be found in this world. It can only be found in and through Him. For in Him do we live, move and have our being (Acts 17:28).

Saved Not Single

Many identify the single person as someone who is lonely, unwanted, and unloved. There are some who believe the single person can only reach a certain height in their career or ministry. I've had numerous people tell me that as I enter pastoral ministry, that now I really need a spouse. While there are plenty of benefits to having a spouse, and I truly do desire one at my current stage of life, not having one will not prevent the Lord from working within my life. My identity is in being *saved not single*. Because I am a believer in Jesus, I live for Him first and foremost. My identity is in Christ.

Ephesians 2:10 makes it clear: "For we are His creation, created in Christ Jesus for good works, which God prepared ahead of time so that we should walk in them." It is evident that all believers were created in Christ Jesus to do a work for Him. Scripture doesn't tell us that we must wait until we're married to do certain things for the Lord. Your relationship status is not a condition to doing work for the kingdom of God. Believers were created in Christ Jesus for good works and in Him alone we discover our identity.

We as a Church have to stop making it seem as if marriage should be the ultimate goal of the believer. My ultimate goal is to love God and to love all people. My primary desire is to glorify Christ and to make Him known. Therefore, whatever helps me accomplish that best, I'm certain the Lord will provide. If that's a wife, then glory to God! If it's not, then glory to God!

If God can use Paul, who was not married, to write most of the New Testament then surely marriage isn't the ultimate goal. Better yet, if God can send His son Jesus, who never married, to die on a cross for our sins and rise again with all power in His hands, then surely marriage isn't the ultimate goal. Marriage is a beautiful thing that can truly represent Christ in a unique way. But the same can be done in the life of an unmarried person. Our identity and purpose are found in Christ, not our relationship status.

Small Group Discussion 1

1. Do you find things such as music, movies, or even social media affecting how you view relationships? If so, how do you prevent yourself from digesting those things?

2. I believe the purpose for dating is to find out if that person is your spouse, and the goal is to glorify God. Do you agree with this? How does this affect who and when you date?

3. Do you feel as if the term "singleness" has carried a negative connotation to it?

2

Undivided Devotion

The ultimate goal for our lives should not be getting married but to follow Jesus and bring glory to His name. Each given day with breath in our lungs is an opportunity to pursue Christ and advance His kingdom. If you don't have Jesus, you will always have an empty life, whether married or unmarried.

Our salvation is not tied to marriage. We are saved only by grace through faith in Jesus. It is by the sacrificial love of Jesus, who died and rose again for our iniquities, that we have access to life and life more abundantly (John 10:10). Whether married or unmarried, I urge you to keep Jesus at the center of your life. We ought to do all things for the glory of God and by the heart of God, meaning we align ourselves to His will and way. We allow the Lord to lead us.

Surrender All to God

In general, I think we as Christians tend to focus too much on receiving than releasing. When I read about Jesus and what it takes to follow Him, all I see are examples of godly self-sacrifice. That's what He demonstrated here on earth. We cannot receive the abundance of what God has for us without first releasing the grip on our own lives. How do we do this? We must take our selfish passions and nail them to the cross. We must take our agendas and nail them to the cross. We have to first deny ourselves and pick-up our cross daily in order to truly follow Jesus.

I believe this is what true worship looks like. Worship is saying, "less of me, more of You." This is our response to our personal relationship with God. If you truly know God and walk with Him, you can't help but surrender. He is simply better than us. He is greater than all things. His plans are better than ours. His ways are better than ours. Therefore, our response should be "more of you, Jesus, and less of me." It's when we decrease ourselves that we truly invite the Lord to have His way in and through our lives.

Many plans are in a man's heart, but the Lord's decree will prevail (Proverbs 19:21). We ought to trust in the Lord with all our heart—leaning not on our own understanding. Allow Him to direct our paths (Proverbs 3:5-6). When God leads us, He doesn't get lost. He knows the way. Trust and know that He has a plan for your future. These plans are to prosper you and not to harm you (Jeremiah 29:11).

Benefits of Being Unmarried

The unmarried have a unique advantage to do whatever helps them serve the Lord best with fewer distractions than those who are married. In 1 Corinthians, the Apostle Paul (an unmarried man) says, "He who is unmarried cares for the things of the Lord—how he may please the Lord. But he who is married cares about the things of the world—how he may please his wife" (1 Corinthians 7:32-33). I'm reluctant to say that distracted devotion to the Lord is a disadvantage to marriage. I would say it's more of a challenge that you must learn to navigate. Your devotion is divided in marriage. You have to please your spouse, but above all, God. The unmarried do not have divided devotion. There are, of course, some unmarried people who have children whether out of wedlock, widowed or divorced. Children, especially when young, are time consuming. However, you too have an opportunity to experience undivided devotion to the Lord. It just takes more intention.

Your gift of undivided devotion to the Lord should greatly benefit His Church. Married people tend to be glorified within the Church and for good reason, marriage is a beautiful thing. However, so is being unmarried, specifically if you're using your unmarried status for the glory of God and the good of others. Use this time to advance the kingdom of God in ways that are more challenging for married people.

You must steward the gift of being unmarried. Whether it's a call for a season or lifetime, your unmarried status has a purpose. Most importantly, you must use this time of being unmarried to grow in faith and to strengthen your relationship with God.

It's so easy to view the season of being unmarried as simply a phase to prepare for a relationship that leads to marriage. Yet, we miss the mark with that mindset. We should be cultivating our relationship with God and seeking Him with our whole heart.

How to Avoid Idleness

I continue to develop in this area as an unmarried young adult. It's easy to become idle and feel lonely as an unmarried person. Loneliness is a feeling that all unmarried people occasionally experience. Idleness can easily be experienced for the one who isn't working toward a goal, utilizing their gifts, doing ministry—being productive. I often find that loneliness and idleness go hand-in-hand.

As a person who grew up an only child, loneliness was never something that made me uncomfortable. I'm very much an introvert, so being alone tends to be a preference of mine in general. However, as I get older, the more that feeling of loneliness becomes an uncomfortable place. There's this longing for companionship that wasn't really there for me prior to the age of twenty-five.

In those moments of feeling lonely, my mind often begins to wonder about things that some peers have that I don't have, like a significant other. I begin to question my path and get down on myself for not having a wife. On one hand, it points to a desire to one day get married. There is nothing wrong with having that desire. However, that sense of loneliness may also point to something deeper, like a feeling of insufficiency in Christ. This is why it's so important that our relationship status doesn't become our identity. Our identity must be in Christ.

Even I have to constantly remind myself that Jesus is not only enough, but *more* than enough. He's all I need. But if I'm being honest, the times I feel most lonely are the times I feel most distant from God. By no means is this a result of God being distant from me. Quite the contrary, it's a result of me being distant from Him.

I've learned that I must draw near. The only way to fill that void is to hunger and thirst for Christ. Only He can truly satisfy. When we draw near to God, He will draw near to us (James 4:8). This is one of many biblical promises God has given us. He is faithful and does not lie.

Being on idle time—not doing anything when you could be doing something—is when I feel loneliness the most. Over the years, I've discovered practical ways that work for me to combat loneliness. One of those ways is pulling out my keyboard and writing worship songs. This helps me stimulate my creative side while simultaneously spending private time with the Lord. When I write worship songs, I spend a significant amount of those sessions studying scripture. Having sound theology is important to me and it helps me desire to study God's Word.

Another way I combat loneliness is by cooking while listening to music or a podcast. I'll be honest, oftentimes there's R&B in my ears when cooking, but I've been intentional with building a playlist that is clean. It helps that my favorite artist is PJ Morton and you never have to worry about vulgarity in his music. Cooking while listening to music or a podcast is literally my favorite thing to do. It's another way of tapping into my creative gene and it helps me decompress.

Although I am an introvert and enjoy being alone, I also love hanging with friends. Hanging with friends reminds me that I am not alone in this life. I have a community of people that I can lean on and do life with. We need community. We need each other.

One of the best ways to combat times of loneliness is by drawing near to the Lord through prayer. This is not merely true for the unmarried, but this is true for the married as well. It's important for the unmarried to understand that a relationship isn't going to cure your loneliness. There are people who are married and just as lonely as they were before getting married. Many times, as I've learned from married friends, this can be attributed to a lack of intimacy with their spouse and that isn't even always in terms of sexual connection.

Intimacy is important in relationships. Likewise, it is important with our relationship with the Lord. We must draw near to Him. Spending time in prayer with God helps align our hearts with His. It's through prayer that we can lay our burdens down and hand over our desires. He is faithful to offer grace and mercy.

When you are diligently seeking God and allowing Him to lead you in His righteousness, you gain peace. So many unmarried people become weary that they will never experience the gift of marriage. Glorify God by seeking Him and His righteousness first. If you do get married one day, He will lead you in the process. But He's not leading those who don't follow Him. When you place matters into your own hands, you remove God from the equation, which can be disastrous. For surely, "the LORD 's blessing enriches, and he adds no painful effort to it (Proverbs 10:22, CSB).

Value Your Time

Another component to loneliness that often gets overlooked by Christians is that while the unmarried have undivided devotion unto God, their relationships with others require extra intention. Unlike married people, those who are unmarried don't have the privilege of going home to their best friend every single day. Even if an unmarried person lives with their best friend, which I hear is quite difficult to do, that is still a relationship that takes extra intention. You're not bonded by a marital covenant.

I bring this up because it's commonplace to have this unsaid expectation that unmarried people have more time to serve the church. On the surface, and as previously stated, that may be true, but that doesn't give the church permission to be inconsiderate of an unmarried person's time. We can't just assume that an unmarried person will always be able to serve at every single church event. Sure they have more ability to experience undivided devotion unto the Lord, however, that doesn't always have to be demonstrated through serving their local church. It's important for the unmarried to also invest time with their community of friends and family. That investment can't simply wait until one gets home. It takes planning time to hangout or talk.

Sometimes it means missing that Friday night church event and instead going out to dinner with friends you haven't seen in a week. Sometimes that means not staying later-than-planned at a midweek church service so that you have time to chat with your friends over the phone. That doesn't make you less godly. If anything, that strengthens your faith-walk. Having a godly community of friends is not only important, but healthy. That is true for both the unmarried and the married. However, an unmarried person needs that godly community even more so than a married person with a spouse to confide in daily.

The Bible tells us to be devoted to one another in love (Romans 12:10). I thank God for my brothers and sisters in Christ. There is truly a blood that is thicker than all other blood and that's the blood of Jesus! Brothers and sisters in Christ are forever family through the precious blood of Jesus.

My godly community of friends is a priority in my life. Some of them are married and some of them are not. Of course, relationships can vary based on marital status, especially with the opposite sex. But my closest sisters in Christ are unmarried. Given the similar circumstance of not being married, our friendships can thrive in ways that it likely won't when married.

Some of my brothers in Christ are married. But one thing they do, which is a testament to their character, is they still make time for us unmarried guys. I think this is great and necessary to have. Married people should be intentional about inviting unmarried friends into their home and hanging out with them.

For the unmarried, stewarding this gift means not only making the most of your freedom to have undivided devotion unto God, but also being free to make the most of your time with others. When you are married, you can still have great friendships with others, but it's undoubtedly going to look different. Your primary relationship is with your spouse. A lot of times that means having boundaries with others. A married person shouldn't simply hang out whenever they want to, they should be considerate of their spouse. A married person shouldn't spend hours on the phone whenever they want to with a friend of the opposite sex. They should be considerate of their spouse. There are many considerations that should take place, in a beautiful way of honoring one another, within the covenant of marriage. However, the unmarried person does not have those same considerations. Sure there may be boundaries you have set for the relationships with your friends. However, you have more freedom. Steward it well.

Use this time of your life to really lean into your friendships. These are necessary relationships that should help hold you accountable and help refine you as a person. Love God and don't forget about loving others.

Small Group Discussion 2

1. Are you using your unmarried status for the glory of God and the good of others? If so, how are you doing that? If not, in what ways do you think you could accomplish that?

2. How do you combat those times of loneliness and idleness?

3. Do you have a godly community of friends? Are you investing intentional time with your family and friends?

3

UNGODLY ADVICE

Personally, maybe the toughest thing about being an unmarried young man is the pressure received from family, friends and the church to be in a relationship. Especially when you are not dating. The advice or criticism people have tried to give me has often been unwarranted, uneducated, and has honestly made me feel uncomfortable.

I have had friends attempt to push me into relationships with ladies that I knew were not for me to pursue. There's been plenty of times where I've had people in my church community roll their eyes when I tell them that I'm not dating. But I think the toughest group I've had to navigate is family. To be honest, some of the criticism I've received from family members has been borderline degrading. There have been numerous occasions where I've even had my sexuality questioned by family members simply because I wasn't dating. This is extremely unhealthy and ungodly behavior. It's ignorance.

We've become so accustomed to what the world says about relationships that we neglect to discover what the Bible says on the subject. Marriage is a good thing. Being unmarried, the apostle Paul even argues, is a better thing. Again, you have an opportunity for undivided devotion to the Lord as an unmarried person. However, Paul writes that not everyone would be able to remain unmarried like him. 1 Corinthians 7:6-9 says this: "I say this as a concession, not as a command. I wish that all people were just like me. But each has his own gift from God, one in this way and another in that way. I say to the unmarried and to widows: It is good for them if they remain as I am. But if they do not have self-control, they should marry, for it is better to marry than to burn with desire."

Paul argues that it is good for the unmarried and widows to remain unmarried. In the previous verses (1 Corinthians 7:1-6), Paul explains some requirements within marriage which could be challenging. He says that both the husband and wife do not have authority over their own bodies within marriage, but that it belongs to each other. Paul mentions that the husband and wife are not to deprive one another from sex. The only exception Paul mentions is when the wife and husband have agreed to set aside sex for a time. This time, Paul says, must be devoted to prayer. He says that this is not a commandment from God. It's also not a recommendation. God has given the married couple freedom to abstain from sex for a brief time and for a spiritual reason. The reason this time of abstaining from sex should be brief is because of self-control, or lack thereof.

These layers in marriage are good things and can be enjoyed. However, they can also be a challenge. So Paul says that he wishes all people could be just like him and remain unmarried. Then he raises an important point that each person carries his own gift from God, one this and another that. Paul is speaking of two gifts here: the gift of remaining unmarried and the gift of marriage.

We must be careful in how we interpret these words from Paul. This verse is often overstated and misinterpreted. I have heard it said more often than not that if you have sexual desires, God has not given you the gift of being unmarried. I think the more accurate way we should state this is, if you have sexual desires, God has made available a gift of marriage in which you can rightly fulfill those desires. Again, just because you have sexual desires does not mean that they must be fulfilled. You must depend on the Lord for strength. It is a constant decision to die to self and find contentment in the Lord.

For the believer, when it comes to sexual temptation, you have two options: get married or remain celibate. However, if you take advantage of this marriage gift, you must first consider the requirements of a *godly* marriage. God's plan for marriage is that one man and one woman become one flesh (Genesis 2:24). We know that as believers we are not to be unequally yoked together with unbelievers (2 Corinthians 6:14). Therefore, in order for the Lord to be glorified in your union, you must be married to a fellow believer.

There are also other considerations if you choose to pursue the gift of marriage, which can sometimes complicate the journey to marriage. It is not often that a person goes from being unmarried to immediately being married. An engagement is the period between those phases. For some, it can be a short time and for others, it can take a little longer.

Many, if not most, believers desire marriage, but there are some who do not. If you fall into that latter category, then much like those who desire marriage, you must consider all of what scripture says is forbidden outside of marriage. The biggest issue at hand is usually sexual temptation. Again, as a believer you have two options: get married and fulfill those sexual desires or remain celibate.

In 1 Corinthians 7:7-9, Paul is not saying that marriage is the only gift. Paul says that being unmarried is a gift and being married is a gift. Therefore, whatever state you find yourself in, it is a gift.

Paul makes it clear that he was not married here in 1 Corinthians 7. However, there are many biblical scholars who believe that Paul could have been married at one point. Scripture does not tell us this one way or another, but scholars believe this because Paul was a devout Jew. In those days, it was considered a sin for a Jewish man to be unmarried past the age of 20. Paul also alluded, though not blatantly, to being a member of the Sanhedrin. You could not be a member of the Sanhedrin unless you were a married man. Therefore, it is possible and likely probable that Paul was married at one time. His wife, if he had one, likely died considering the fact that Paul never mentions her in his writings.

If Paul was married at one time, he would have experienced both the gift of marriage and the gift of being single. I mention this because scripture also doesn't speak to the permanency of either gift. Though it does speak of reasons to end a marriage (Matthew 5:31-32). It was never God's intention for marriage to end in divorce. Although being unmarried or married are both gifts that God gives, it is not grouped with the spiritual gifts listed in 1 Corinthians 12. We have all experienced the gift of singleness at some point in our lives. Therefore, I believe that the state of being unmarried is a gift that God gives everyone, at least temporarily. There are some who accept the gift of being unmarried as permanent. There are others who trade in their gift of being unmarried for the gift of being married.

As for me, I currently have the gift of being single. Why? Because your boy is not yet married! I greatly desire marriage and a family of my own. However, until that day comes, I have been given a gift of being unmarried and I must steward this season of my life well.

If you are single, view it as a gift. The Lord will provide you with all you need to live a life devoted to loving Him and loving His people. He will keep you from falling into sin as an unmarried person if you rely on Him for strength.

Of course, Paul also says, "if they do not have self-control, they should marry, for it is better to marry than to burn with desire." Paul isn't drawing a hard line and saying that you must marry if you are tempted sexually. He's saying this is a good reason to marry.

I have plenty married friends who have told me that sexual temptation doesn't just all of a sudden disappear when you get married. In fact, it's often magnified. Therefore, if self-control is not developed outside of marriage, it will become an issue even when you are married. We often forget that self-control is a fruit of the spirit and it is not typically easy. But God is faithful if we lean on Him for strength.

So while Paul says it is a good reason for the person who does not have self-control to marry, he is not giving permission for you to not have self-control. He is simply saying that it is better for you to marry and fulfill those desires than to burn with those desires.

Again, this marriage must be in line with God's design for it. For many, finding a spouse does not happen overnight. However, God is able to sustain you as an unmarried person and He is able to sustain you as a married person. We must lean on Him and rely on Him in both situations.

The Three Eunuchs

Jesus also has much to say about this subject. In Matthew 19, the Pharisees tried to test Jesus by asking what they thought was a trick question. But, of course, people can't trick Jesus! Their questions were in regard to divorce and if it's lawful to divorce on any grounds. Jesus responds by quoting Old Testament Scripture, then He says, "Whoever divorces his wife, except for sexual immorality, and marries another, commits adultery." His disciples, responded by saying, "If the relationship of a man with his wife is like this, it's better not to marry!" Then Jesus said, "not everyone can accept this saying, but only those it has been given to" (Matthew 19:9-11). Sounds familiar? It would appear that Paul was echoing Jesus' words in 1 Corinthians 7.

Jesus proceeds to list three types of eunuchs: in this context meaning a eunuch is one who is unable to have sex and produce children. Therefore, the eunuch goes against the cultural norm, remains unmarried, and celibate. Jesus says in Matthew 19:12 (NASB), "There are eunuchs who were born that way from their mother's womb; and there are eunuchs who were made by people; and there are eunuchs who have made themselves that way because of the kingdom of heaven."

Two of those eunuchs that Jesus lists are eunuchs involuntarily. The third eunuch that Jesus lists makes Himself that way for a spiritual purpose. Jesus ends His statement by saying, "let anyone accept this who can." Essentially, Jesus is saying to embrace the gift of being unmarried. He's not saying that you should never marry or desire to get married. But He's saying that if you are single, accept it and make the most of it. Being unmarried is a gift and an opportunity to do good work for the kingdom of God. However, the antagonizing behavior of pushing a person to marry has to stop. The state of being unmarried is a gift. For some, it's a lifelong calling. It is God-ordained. What you're really doing is advising against God's Word when you speak wrongly into an unmarried person's life. We must be careful.

I know for most it's coming from a place of love. You want your loved one to experience the beauty of marriage. But again, let's not assume that being unmarried can't be beautiful. The glorious Gospel applies to both the unmarried and married. God can use you with or without a spouse. We should never question the unmarried brother or sister who is pursuing God wholeheartedly. That undivided devotion serves a major purpose in advancing His kingdom, just as it does for those with divided devotion.

We should encourage our unmarried brothers and sisters to continue standing on their convictions. If the Holy Spirit has placed in their heart not to pursue marriage for some time, hold them accountable. Help them through the highs and lows of this unmarried season. Keep them in prayer. But don't degrade these individuals by making them seem any less than those who are under the covenant of marriage. Don't push them towards pursuing a relationship because you think they're running out of time or need a spouse. Christ is all we need. His timing and ways are perfect.

To the unmarried, I urge you to stand firm. Sometimes you will have to draw the sword, that being the Word of God, to combat ungodly advice or criticism. Above all, obey God. Don't allow anyone to make you feel marginalized or inadequate. Again, the same Gospel that applies to the married also applies to the unmarried. Jesus Christ loved us all enough to die for our sin and shame. He rose again so that we may all have life and life more abundantly in Him. Christ is enough and He doesn't love you any more or less based on your relationship status.

Other Culture

Another layer to this is that sometimes the promotion of relationships gets hammered into you at a young age. Children are dating in elementary school now because it's a mindset they learned early. Honestly, it's perversion, and it has creeped into youth because of unwise and ungodly promotion of relationships. Whether intentional or unintentional, this is happening and it's dangerous. It also doesn't help that the idea of worldly relationship behavior is more accessible now than ever through social media and the internet. It's all around us, but it is important to protect youth from digesting ungodly and inappropriate relationship behavior. Protect their innocence and lead them in the ways of the Lord.

As Christians, we are not to be of the culture. We really shouldn't even be counterculture. We ought to be "other culture." Jesus, in His sermon on the mount, did not merely take culture and flip it upside down. Jesus took culture and established His own. Culture says not to murder is enough. Jesus says don't act or speak out of anger. Culture defines adultery as sex between a married and an unmarried person. Jesus says that simply looking at a person with lust in your heart already makes you guilty of adultery. Culture says to treat evil with evil. Jesus says, not only to treat them with love, but to go an extra mile.

Kingdom culture is not counterculture, it's another culture. Those who are not in Christ will never be able to understand, nor be able to accomplish what Jesus taught in that sermon on the mount. Christians can't even accomplish it without His help and guidance through the Holy Spirit. Therefore, do not become stained by worldly culture. Likewise, do not take what is from the culture and attempt to make it more holy. Only Jesus is holy. Follow Him and His ways.

It will not be easy to do this. It's why we must lean on Jesus for strength. Worldly culture is around us 24/7. Whether it's through social media or in-person conversations, there just seems to be so many expectations. If we allow culture to influence us, we would believe if we're not married by a certain age, something is wrong with us. If we don't have kids by a certain age, there's something wrong. There are expectations for when you should have your own house or apartment, when you should lose your virginity, when you should fully be inserted into a career and so much more. It has placed this imaginary clock in our heads that says we're not where we should be in life; and maybe for some that's true. Maybe you could have those things, but you don't, all because of your lack of action. People often try to blame their lack of these things on God, but He never promised any of that for us in scripture. What He does promise is His presence, guidance, strength, grace and mercy.

We are not told in scripture that we ought to be married at a certain age or have kids by a certain age. Abraham's wife Sarah didn't even have a child until she was 90 or 91 years old! (Genesis 17:17, 18:10). I'm not saying God would perform that same miracle today, but the point is, God is going to accomplish what His will is for your life if you trust Him.

The Bible says that those who know to do right and don't are in sin (James 4:17). That is the very definition of faith without works being dead. How do we know what is right for us to do? Surely it isn't by culture. It isn't even by our own wisdom. It is by the wisdom that only comes from the Lord. This is when the Lord's desires begin to overpower your desires and you start to walk in *His* will. It's not a recipe to receive what you want. This is the design God has given us to begin to align our hearts with His. The world will never be able to understand it. Our human minds will never be able to fully grasp it, but it's by Christ that we are able to decipher what is right for us to do. When this happens, we can live in a culture and not be stained by it.

Small Group Discussion 3

1. Have you ever received ungodly relationship advice from friends or family? How did you deal with that?

2. Do you view being unmarried as a gift?

3. What are some ways you can steward self-control outside of marriage?

4

BE FAITHFUL

If there's any advice I can give to the unmarried Christian who desires to one day get married, it is to be faithful with the relationships you have now. We are told in Luke 12:48 that "From everyone who has been given much, much will be demanded; and from the one who has been entrusted with much, much more will be asked." Many people view these words from Jesus as being specifically for those with wealth, but that is not so.

First of all, what greater wealth is there than to know and be known by Jesus? What greater gift is there than the grace given freely unto us by Jesus? Regardless of your economic state, if you have Jesus, you have much. If the Lord has given you family, it is plenty. If you have friends, it is much. If you have gifts and talents, that comes from the Lord, generously. Even regarding wealth, that too comes from the Lord. Therefore, we must steward those things well.

Whatever we have in the season we are in can be used to bring God glory and be for the good of God's people.

As an unmarried young adult, one of the things I've tried to do is be faithful to my family and friends. Habits while single won't automatically change once you get married. In fact, I'm sure they get magnified when married. Therefore, why not build healthy habits prior to marriage?

I feel like my family dynamic is a little unique, especially since the passing of my grandfather. I've had to take on the role as the "man of the family" and it's something I take seriously. My grandfather was always dependable and there for our family. I always admired that about him and have tried my best to display those same qualities.

My mom comes from a blended family, as my grandfather had three children from a previous marriage (one of them being my mom) and my non-biological grandmother (who I simply refer to as grandma) had two children from a previous marriage. My mom was the only daughter of the bunch and also the only one who really has done something with her life.

I grew up the only child of an unmarried mother. So now as an adult, with the inconsistent presence of my uncles, I'm the lone man of the family. After my grandfather died in 2018 (really a couple years prior to that because of his health), I had to step up and be there for my mom and grandmother.

In 2020, my mom reconnected with her biological mother. Prior to 2020, their relationship was not great. Therefore, my relationship with my biological grandmother (who I refer to as Grandma Lil) was rather nonexistent. But in 2020, the Lord brought reconciliation to our relationship with her. We would go out to Baltimore where she lived to check on her during the pandemic but quickly realized there was a serious issue. She was a hoarder and for a while we thought that was the main problem with Grandma Lil. However, as we continued to visit her home in Baltimore we began to notice that there was more going on. So we devised a plan to bring her to our home permanently and find her a new doctor. After several tests and doctor appointments we learned that Grandma Lil had Alzheimer's-dementia (and likely had it for a while), among other medical problems.

Isn't it amazing how God works though? The year 2020 was wild for everyone worldwide. But had it not been for the pandemic, I'm not sure that my mom and grandma Lil would have reconciled. If it had not been for the reconciliation, I'm not sure we would have known the issues she was having. So I thank God for weaving His goodness in such a troubling time.

By 2021, not only had my mom and I discovered that my grandma Lil had Alzheimer's-dementia, along with other medical issues, but we also realized that my grandmother (non-biological) was having some memory issues. Maybe the biggest sign for us realizing my grandmother was having memory issues is that she would get confused driving. This concerned me greatly because I actually remember a conversation that I had with my grandfather in 2017. He had raised some concerns about my grandmother not remembering how to get home one day from a generally routine outing. My grandfather wasn't driving much at that point due to his health, so that alerted me to make sure my mom and I ran more errands for them. I didn't immediately tell my mother about that conversation because I didn't want to add additional worry as my grandfather was battling cancer, but that conversation came back to my mind in 2021 when those memory lapses became more prevalent every time my grandmother would drive somewhere. At that point, I told my mom about the conversation I had with my grandfather back in 2017 and we began to limit where my grandmother would drive. She still had her vehicle and could drive to the grocery store up the road from her house, as that was generally not a route in which she'd get lost.

The final straw came mid-2021 when I ordered an Uber for my grandmother's hair appointment. The plan was for Uber to pick her up from her house and then a close friend of the family would take her home from the hair salon. My mom and I both had to work. So I set up her transportation thinking that would be a good plan for her to get from point A to point B and back. However, that plan went terribly wrong.

My grandmother was picked up by Uber and I intentionally used the app to track the vehicle's movement. I also used the chat to communicate to the driver that my grandmother would likely not remember where her hair salon is located but to please follow the address given to him. No more than 7 minutes into what would've been a 15 minute drive, I saw the vehicle going the wrong direction. It ended up stopping at a completely different location and the app tracker shut off. My grandmother had forgotten to bring her cell phone that day, so I lost all communication. Due to the app shutting off, I barely knew exactly where she was. So, of course, worry began to rise.

Based on the knowledge I had of where the vehicle stopped, I called businesses that were in the vicinity asking if they had seen my grandmother. After no success, I immediately called 911. Then I called the friend of our family who was going to take my grandmother home. I asked her to just drive in the general area to see if she could find my grandmother. There was no success with the police and there was no success with our family friend.

An hour or so went by and just as I was headed to search for her, my grandmother rang our doorbell. She knew that my mom and I were working from home and remembered our address. It shocked me to see her at the door. It definitely brought great relief to see her, but my head was spinning because I didn't understand what happened. I am forever thankful for whoever the Uber driver was, because he went above and beyond his duties. He told me that she insisted her hair salon was in a different location. When she realized it wasn't in that location, she became distraught because she didn't know where she was. So she had the driver bring her to my house. The driver did all of this without proper compensation. Even when he came to my house and I tried to compensate him more, he refused. I truly believe God was working through that man.

When my grandmother came into the house, she was in great distress. So my mom and I let her sit for a while and essentially grieve what just happened. Then I had to assume my position as man of the family and decide at that very moment to let her know she would no longer be allowed to drive. Next to my grandfather's death only three years prior, this moment was the toughest I have ever faced in my life. As a 28 year old, I had to tell my grandmother that she could no longer drive. Not only that, but I would be coming to take her car.

I took her home that day and grabbed her car keys, though I hadn't yet moved the car, as I wanted to allow her some time to heal from all that had just transpired. Several days later my mom and I went to get my grandmother's car. I had a plan to not only pick up the car, but to take my grandmother on a ride and explain to her again why I had to take the car. I really wrestled with this because on one hand, I felt like the bad guy. I was literally not only stopping my grandmother from driving but also taking away her car. On the other hand, I knew that this needed to be done.

So I prayed on it. I asked God for strength and wisdom. I wanted to make sure when I took my grandmother on this ride that I would display compassion, empathy, sympathy and love. I can sometimes come across as nonchalant when leading my family because I try to be careful with putting my emotions on display. Not in an unhealthy way, but in a way that lets them know everything will be okay. But I do realize that it can come across as nonchalant or cold, so I try to be careful. This is why it was crucial for me to pray for strength and wisdom.

I ended up taking my grandmother on this ride and I just asked her to direct me to her hair salon. For a minute there, she thought she knew where the hair salon was, but much like that Uber drive, she pointed out the wrong direction. I ended up driving her to the actual location of her hair salon and just stopped for a minute to let her know this is why I had to take her car. I told her that she had been showing signs for a long time that her memory while driving was not good. I told her how dangerous that can be and has been for her. Then I reiterated how my mom and I would be there for her and how much we love her.

On the way back to drop her off at home, I allowed her to just process everything. We didn't talk much on the way home. She did a little bit of crying but mostly processing. When we reached her house, she told me how thankful she is for my mom and me. She also told me how proud my grandfather would be of me in that moment and that she knows the decision is what's best. That really encouraged me. As a young black man who now carried this responsibility to be there for his family, it is a weight that often feels too heavy. I often don't know how to handle things or what to do, and I often feel incapable and discouraged. It also triggers grief, as I know these are things my grandfather would have handled if he was alive. God had to remind me in the moment, that because I leaned on Him for strength and guidance, I was on the right path. He had to remind me that I was doing the right thing.

I mention all of this to hammer home a point that my family needed me and I was able to be there 100% for them. Lord willing, there will be a day when I am married and my wife becomes my top priority. I will still remain responsible for my mom and grandmothers, along with the family I'll be building. Until that day comes, however, I must be faithful to the family I have now. I'm certain this will help prepare me for my future family. So I'm thankful for where the Lord currently has me and what He has given me.

I am reminded of the story of Ruth. I feel like many refer to Ruth and Boaz when discussing that book of the bible. However, there's another great relationship that is described in that book and it's between Ruth and Naomi.

In Ruth 1, we see that Naomi had just gone through the ringer. There was a famine in Israel which caused Naomi, her husband and two sons to move. Scripture says that they moved to Moab and settled there. But Naomi's husband, Elimelech died and she was left with their two sons, Chillion and Mahlon. Each son took a Moabite woman as a wife, one named Orpah and the other Ruth. They lived in Moab for about 10 years before both Chillion and Mahlon died. This left Naomi now without her husband and sons.

So Naomi returned to Israel bitterly. She deemed herself too old to have another husband. Not only that, but she deemed herself too old to bear children. Initially both Ruth and Orpah were traveling back to Israel with Naomi. But Naomi presented an out for both Orpah and Ruth, "She said to them, 'Each of you go back to your mother's home. May the Lord show faithful love to you as you have shown to the dead and to me. May the Lord enable each of you to find security in the house of your new husband.' She kissed them, and they wept loudly. 'No,' they said to her. 'We will go with you to your people.' But Naomi replied, 'Return home, my daughters. Why do you want to go with me? Am I able to have any more sons who could become your husbands? Return home, my daughters. Go on, for I am too old to have another husband. Even if I thought there was still hope for me to have a husband tonight and to bear sons, would you be willing to wait for them to grow up? Would you restrain yourselves from remarrying? No, my daughters, my life is much too bitter for you to share, because the Lord 's hand has turned against me'" (Ruth 1:8-13).

Naomi told both Orpah and Ruth that there would be nothing for them in Judah. They were not obligated to go to Israel with their mother-in-law and Naomi wanted to make that clear. So the scripture says that Orpah kissed Naomi, indicating that she would return to Moab. Yet, Ruth clung to Naomi. She didn't have to, but she chose to stay with Naomi. Not only that, but Ruth makes a vow, "For wherever you go, I will go, and wherever you live, I will live; your people will be my people, and your God will be my God. Where you die, I will die, and there I will be buried. May Yahweh punish me, and do so severely, if anything but death separates you and me" (Ruth 1:16-17).

That's an incredible picture of loyalty. Ruth was loyal to Naomi, even though she wasn't obligated. Not only that, but the Lord also blessed Ruth through her decision to stay with Naomi. Ruth went on to marry, you know, that guy named Boaz. Together they bore a son, Obed, who would become grandfather to King David. So by God's sovereignty, not only did God bless Ruth but He would change the landscape of world history through her. We may not know why God has us in the situation we are in right now, but rest assured, God has a reason and plan. We need merely to trust and obey Him. Ruth displayed true loyalty. She showed love, compassion and friendship to Naomi. I think there is wisdom in this for how we should be loyal to God and His people.

Ruth made sacrifices to leave her homeland. But God ultimately blessed her greatly and weaved His plan for the world through her in the process. What a mighty God we serve!

Prioritize your family. If you have parents and siblings or close family members in your life, pour into them, spend time with them. Realize that your family is your first ministry, even if you are not married. Your family should get the first of your time and energy, not the leftovers. So often, especially in America, we find ourselves prioritizing our work. It's super easy for us to become workaholics. It is very good for us to work and to do our jobs well. However, we have to set boundaries around that and make sure we create room to steward those other areas of our life. Even as ministry leaders, it can be so easy for us to pour out everything to the church, so that we have nothing left for our family. Be present for your family and give them your best.

This will be so essential when and if you are ever to marry. You should not be absent in the lives of your spouse and children. If you are, it will greatly impact those relationships. Let's look at our relationship with God for example. If we do not spend time with God through His word and prayer, our relationship with Him will suffer. In fact, our relationship with others will suffer as well because in that scenario we are failing to allow God to fuel us. Though none of us will ever be perfect at this—thank God for His faithfulness—this is a requirement to the life of a believer. Likewise, we must prioritize the relationship with our family.

Be faithful to your friends too. Having friends is such a blessing. While I prioritize my family I also make time for my friends as well. This balance is really important. Friendships can help you grow if you're surrounding yourself with the right people. Spend time with your friends. Be a listening ear when they need it, encourage them, seek counsel from them, and learn from them.

I find that both family and friends can really help foster one of the more important things needed in a marriage: communication. All my married friends have mentioned communication as one of the most important aspects of their marriage. That can be fostered before marriage in your relationship with family and friends. Communicate with them, tell them what's on your mind and be transparent. Become a good listener! Not only that but learn to argue well. Learn to respect the other person with your words and deeds.

There is so much that God can be doing through us and for us even while unmarried. We may not see it now, but we must trust Him. He is developing and shaping our character. He is probably using our family and friends to reveal areas of our life that we need to adjust. We may not know what the Lord is doing, but we ought to have confidence in Him. We must follow His leading and steward well what He has given.

Small Group Discussion 4

1. Are you faithful with your current non-romantic relationships? Do you have boundaries in those relationships?

2. Do you find it hard to trust the Lord and His plan when you can't see it?

3. Do you have boundaries in your personal life? What are they and do you stick to them?

5

Be Content

There are days when I'm super content in my unmarried season and days when I am not. I'll be honest, as I get older, those days of discontentment have become more frequent. It's something I have to wrestle with and give to God daily. To desire and pursue marriage is a beautiful thing. It's not a sin to desire or pursue marriage, nor does it mean you are being discontented. In fact, it does require putting action to your faith. We should have faith that God will lead us in this area of life, but that doesn't mean we sit around and wait for someone to come knocking on our door. We can put action to our faith by seeking people to date. Although, we should be wise in how we go about exploring options to date.

Some people may intentionally attend conferences, events, or get plugged into a ministry at church to meet people who they could potentially date. There's nothing wrong with that. Some may opt for the more modern approach through online dating or even matchmaking. Those things are not sinful and it does not mean you're being discontented, but it can become sinful and indicate discontentment.

We must be careful not to allow our desire for marriage to overtake us. Remember, getting married should not be the ultimate goal of the believer. Loving God and loving all people should be the ultimate goal of the believer. The most important relationship we have is our relationship with God. Nothing should come before that. I love how 1 John ends in chapter 5, verse 21: "Little children, guard yourselves from idols." Again, desiring marriage is a good thing, but just like anything that is good, if it becomes your ultimate focus, it has become an idol. We must guard ourselves.

It's so easy as an unmarried person to become discontent with where we are in life. It may seem like all your peers are married or in a relationship that may lead to marriage. This can often make the unmarried person believe they're behind in life. It can really fan that flame of desire to get married. This can create something within our hearts that makes the idea of marriage consume us. Instead of going to church to be among the body of Christ and to commune with the Lord, you go with the ultimate goal of finding a spouse. You may go to every conference that comes in your area, not to develop and learn, but with the ultimate goal of finding a spouse. Or, you may become addicted to that online dating app, constantly searching for someone to date because marriage has consumed your mind. We must guard ourselves from idols.

The desire to marry can quickly become an idol if we don't submit that desire to the Lord. That desire can become the god in our life if we are not careful. Idolatry can prevent us from a real relationship with Jesus and damage our relationships with other believers.

I have found that maybe the greatest way discontent shows itself is covetousness. Scripture categorizes covetousness as a form of idolatry, which is a sin. In fact, "do not covet" is one of the ten commandments given to Moses in the Old Testament. Jealousy and envy are things that trigger covetousness. Lusting after what you don't have or greatly desiring a life that someone else has is a form of covetousness. If I'm being honest, this is so easy to fall into as an unmarried person. There can be so much pressure from family, friends and even culture to get married that it overtakes us. It can become the ultimate thing in our lives. It can be all we think about and it can be all we work toward. We must wrestle against this and give it to God.

As believers, we must put to death what belongs to our worldly nature. This includes, as Scripture says: sexual immorality, impurity, lust, evil desire and greed, which is idolatry. Again, lusting after what you don't have or greatly desiring a life that someone else has is a form of covetousness. "So if you have been raised with Christ, seek the things above, where Christ is, seated at the right hand of God. Set your minds on things above, not on earthly things. For you died, and your life is hidden with Christ in God. When Christ, who is your life, appears, then you also will appear with him in glory. Therefore, put to death what belongs to your earthly nature: sexual immorality, impurity, lust, evil desire, and greed, which is idolatry. Because of these, God's wrath is coming upon the disobedient, and you once walked in these things when you were living in them" (Colossians 3:1-7, CSB).

I think as Christians our eyes tend to wander. We tend to focus on worldly things and our eyes tend to covet what we don't currently have. It's a lustful eye and we are all subject to it. This may show itself in different ways. It may be a sneaker that you don't have, don't need and can't really afford, but you desire it so much that you purchase it. The purchase ends up resulting in not being able to pay the bills. Was the sneaker worth that kind of sacrifice? Likely not. It could also be desiring sexual fulfillment outside of its God-ordained entity, marriage. So you try to find fulfillment in porn or sex outside wedlock.

This reminds me of the story where King David covets another man's wife, Bathsheba. He fell into covetousness, which showed itself in the form of lust. David lusted after Bathsheba, slept with her and impregnated her, then had her husband killed (2 Samuel 11-12). Covetousness led David down that sinful path. We must be careful and guard our hearts. It's not easy, especially for the unmarried person. In fact, it's not easy for the *married* person. David was married, many times according to scripture, yet he still fell into covetousness.

If covetousness is not dealt with during the single years, it can become a problem when one does finally marry, leading to devastating consequences for the spouse and family. Thankfully, the Lord has provided us with a better way. Scripture tells us to "seek what is above" (Colossians 3:2).

Matthew 6:33 tells us that we must "seek first the kingdom of God and His righteousness, and all these things will be provided for you." That phrase, "all these things" points to worries that we may have, what we will eat, what we will drink, what tomorrow holds, when we will get married…who we will marry.

We must not mistake this as God handing us everything we want. God will provide what we need and not always what we want. Again, he does this for His glory and the good of His people. But in order for us to align with God's plan for our lives, we must seek Him. Our eyes must stay fixed on Him. For if we don't fix our eyes on Him, we will easily become concerned about what we don't have.

1 Timothy 6:6-9 says this in regard to covetousness, "But godliness with contentment is a great gain. For we brought nothing into the world, and we can take nothing out. But if we have food and clothing, we will be content with these." Godliness with contentment is key! If we have Jesus, we have all we need. Having Jesus alone is enough. He is *Jehovah Jireh* and He makes provision for our needs. It is a promise He keeps. That doesn't mean we will always get what we want, but the Lord does provide what we need. Due to the fact that we are not all-knowing like Jesus, we may even have a false view of what we need. God knows exactly what we need. Therefore, we must trust Him and be thankful for what we do have.

The Lord is going to do what's best for His glory and the good of His people. If you find yourself in the season of being unmarried and you desire to one day be married, find contentment in God. Understand that whatever season you find yourself in should not be wasted. For some people, being unmarried isn't even a season but a lifetime calling. Regardless of where you find yourself, God is working in your life just as He is working in the married person's life.

I have to remind myself nearly every day to be content. There are dating couples and married couples all around me. Not to mention, social media is flooded with dating and married couples. It's also flooded with videos and pictures of extremely attractive women. It's so easy to look at those couples and fall into covetousness. It's also so easy to covet the women that so often pop up on social media. However, I have to wrestle against these things overtaking my mind. It can literally become all I think about and it can be my main desire, but I'm thankful for friends who know this and encourage me in this season of my life.

I'm also intentional about placing boundaries in my life to guard myself from covetousness. Filtering my social media or even staying off social media at times is helpful. Making sure that I stay plugged into my community of friends and family – not isolating myself – also helps. Most importantly, making sure I pray and constantly lift up the desire before God really provides the strength needed to not become discontent. Again, the desire to marry is a good thing. The desire to have sex is also a good thing. God designed both. The more I pursue God above all things, the more I'm reminded of just how much I already have. In this, I must be content.

So I encourage the unmarried person to find contentment in Christ. If you do not find contentment within your unmarried state, you are unlikely to be content if you marry.

Remind yourself of what you do have. Do you have food and water? Do you have family and friends? Do you have clothes on your back and a roof over your head? Are your bills able to be paid? Some people have all those things and some have only a few of those things. Regardless of where you find yourself, if you have God, you have enough.

Desire the Lord above all things. Seek Him through His Word and prayer. Walk with Him. Lay your concerns at His feet. He is faithful to provide what we need. Not always what we want and not always what we *think* we need, but the Lord is faithful to provide what we need.

Small Group Discussion 5

1. Do you battle with discontentment? If so, how do you combat that?

2. Have you made marriage an idol?

3. Do you find yourself coveting what you do not have? If so, how do you combat that?

6

Be Prayerful

Prayer is vital to every believer's life. It can become so easy to undervalue prayer and to think that it can become boring over time. However, prayer is essential. Prayer is the way we communicate with God. Through prayer we can express our gratitude, lift up our worries, align ourselves to the will of God and repent. It is a beautiful act of worship that we so desperately need to utilize every single day.

This is something I need to improve as well. As an unmarried black man, I find myself needing to pray more and more. Especially as I get older. I have experienced the Lord lift the weight of discontent and worry from my heart. I have experienced Him killing fleshly desires and aligning my heart with His. The Lord is more than capable of doing these things if we humbly ask that of Him. But we must humbly ask that of Him through prayer.

Being unmarried already carries its own weight. I absolutely have moments where I do become discouraged and worry about what tomorrow holds. I wonder if I will ever meet the right person and one day get married. I also have self-deprecating moments where I criticize myself. There are moments where I'm wondering why I haven't met the right person. There have definitely been moments of discontentment where I have to remind myself that God is enough. But also, as a black man, I have experienced trauma.

It has become the norm to see black people experience racism and even get killed unjustly. I have experienced racism plenty and to see this stuff still happen grieves my heart. As a person who grew up as an only child, I've always wanted a big family of my own. But I'll be honest that I do occasionally worry about bringing more black kids into this world. They will enter this world with a target on their back. They will not experience life on a fair playing field. These are legitimate concerns that I have considered. However, these are concerns and worries that I must continue to lay at the feet of Jesus.

I want to offer three prayers to unmarried believers. These prayers can certainly also benefit the married believer, but I understand the weight that many unmarried Christians carry. I understand the worries, the concerns, the fears, the sadness and pain. There are plenty more kinds of prayers you can pray, but I wanted to make a concise list.

Prayer 1: "Search My Heart, Oh God"

Psalms 139:23-24 says this: "Search me, God, and know my heart; test me and know my concerns. See if there is any offensive way in me; lead me in the everlasting way." This is a powerful prayer to pray. It's also a dangerous prayer because it's a prayer that the Lord will answer. The Lord will reveal any offensive way in our hearts if we ask that of Him. We have to be ready to repent and turn away from those ways when the Lord does reveal them.

I believe this is a prayer the unmarried person must pray because there can often be offensive ways in our hearts. There are times when we are not placing our hope and trust in the Lord. We can easily fall into the trap of idolizing marriage and falling into discontentment. There are also some unmarried people who may begin to idolize the opposite end of the spectrum: independence. There are some people who idolize being alone and living a life that serves only themselves. That is not God's intention for the believer and it is not His intention for an unmarried person. The freedoms found in being unmarried are not for self-indulgence. We are merely free to love God and love others in a beautifully unique way.

There are also many temptations the unmarried person faces. Lust is often a major issue we must wrestle with. Not only as an unmarried person must we wrestle with lust, but also within marriage. However, it can often present itself in more challenging ways as unmarried people. We must pray for this. We must pray that the Lord reveals the wicked ways of our heart and leads us in His ways.

Prayer

Father, I thank You for being a God we can communicate directly with through prayer. I thank You for being a God who hears and responds to the prayers of Your people. Lord, I lift up every unmarried believer who struggles with discontentment, idolatry and lustful thoughts. I pray that You help dethrone those idols in our lives. I pray that you strengthen the unmarried to flee from sexual temptation. You are the King of kings and the Lord of lords, and all that we can ever need and more is found in You. I pray You do a work on the heart of every unmarried believer, that You begin to reveal every offensive way in our hearts and lead us in Your ways; lead us in Your truth. Test and know the concerns of Your people, for we know that You are a great Comforter. Peace is found in You. Grace and mercy are found in You. You are able to strengthen and guide us. Have Your way in our hearts. Amen.

Prayer 2: "Don't Let Me Wander from Your Commands"

Psalms 119:9-11 says: "How can a young man keep his way pure? By keeping Your word. I have sought You with all my heart; don't let me wander from Your commands. I have treasured Your word in my heart so that I may not sin against You."

This is another important prayer. Psalms 119 is the longest chapter in the bible and it's all about the importance of God's holy Word. The unmarried must hunger and thirst for the Word of God. They must delight in Scripture and all it entails. When we treasure God's Word in our hearts, it helps us to not sin against Him.

Much like our prayer life, however, we can often neglect to read and meditate upon Scripture. Just as we need food, we need spiritual food. We must feast upon it. When you find yourself weak and weary, you can find strength through God's holy Word. When you find yourself struggling with purity, hold on to God's Word. When our eyes become fixated on that which is worthless compared to God, which is all things, we find life through His Word. When we find ourselves without direction and without hope, we must delight in His Word.

I'm afraid as unmarried people, we tend to focus so much on preparing for a future relationship that we neglect to cultivate our relationship with the Lord. I've been guilty of this. I've found myself spending countless hours on YouTube and listening to podcasts, trying to prepare myself for a future relationship. Yet, I would fail to seek the Lord through His holy Word. I would spend more time hearing from others than I would hear from the Lord through Scripture. Flawed views on being unmarried absolutely stem from an insufficient emphasis placed on the Bible. We must be careful. We must follow God's words over man's words.

Prayer

Lord, I thank You for supplying us with the greatest resource known to man - Your holy Word. Help us to delight in it. Help us to hold on to it. Lord, I pray for the unmarried who may struggle with purity and who may find themselves often weary. Strengthen them with Your mighty hand and through Your holy Word. Remind them of Your love, grace and mercy. Father, I also pray that the unmarried fix their eyes on You and away from worthless things. Remind them that You are the great I Am. Remind them that You are sovereign and providential. Remind them that all hope is found in You and it is a hope that is absolute. For we know that although wickedness and suffering may be happening all around us, we can find peace by keeping our eyes set on You. Help us not wander from your Word, Lord, but draw us nearer and nearer. Amen.

Prayer 3: "If the Lord Wills"

James 4:13-17 says: "Come now, you who say, 'Today or tomorrow we will travel to such and such a city and spend a year there and do business and make a profit.' You don't even know what tomorrow will bring — what your life will be! For you are like smoke that appears for a little while, then vanishes. Instead, you should say, 'If the Lord wills, we will live and do this or that.' But as it is, you boast in your arrogance. All such boasting is evil. So it is a sin for the person who knows to do what is good and doesn't do it."

Believing that we can accomplish things outside the will of the Lord is arrogance. Scripture considers such boasting evil. As Christians, we know what we should be doing. "Thy will be done" (Matthew 26:39, KJV) should be the anthem of our lives. Yet, "my will be done" is the refrain we so often struggle with using. This may point to a lack of patience and trust in the Lord.

We live in a microwave culture. We're able to order food from the comfort of our homes and have it delivered to our porch. We don't even have to grocery shop anymore as people can shop and bring it to us. When we want something, it's becoming easier to obtain it. However, some may feel that trusting in the Lord's will is like living in the unknown. You may feel uncomfortable driving down this road we call life with your hands off the wheel and your foot off the pedal. We want what we want and we want it in a timely manner. So we tend to make many plans and form expectations around them. Yet, we don't know what tomorrow holds. Tomorrow is not even guaranteed. But the Lord knows what tomorrow holds because He's holding it. We must trust Him.

We can present our plans and desires to the Lord. But ultimately, the Lord's plans will prevail. Therefore, when we pray, we must align our heart with His. We must trust His sovereignty.

I've prayed this prayer plenty as an unmarried person, "If it's Your will, Lord." I went on a date with a woman once whom I thought was attractive, but I wasn't sure how much I actually liked her. Honestly, I didn't even label this as a date. I jokingly told some friends that this was more of an interest meeting as I needed to figure out just how interested I was in the woman.

Considering how great a desire it was and still is for me to be in a relationship, I was ready to overlook red flags when we went out. But before I met up with this woman, I stopped and prayed. I remember praying, "If it is not Your will for me to date this woman, Lord, make it clear," and surely He did make it clear. While the outing with this woman wasn't horrible, there were plenty of red flags that went up. Yet, part of me still wanted to overlook those things. I really wrestled with this because she was attractive. But God gave me warning after warning and it was up to me at that point to either heed Him or not. Ultimately, I surrendered to the Lord. By no means was that easy though! The Lord will accomplish what He wants to accomplish and no one can get in the way of that. But He allows us to partner with Him by aligning ourselves to His will and way.

There are also things the Lord allows. We may not understand why He allows them, but we must trust Him. We must trust that the Lord will do what's best for His glory and the good of His people. He is a faithful God and we ought to have confidence in Him, for He never fails.

Prayer

God, I thank You for being a faithful God. I'm thankful that no matter what happens around us, it will never prevent You from accomplishing Your will and way. I'm thankful that no matter how much we sin and fall short, that You still remain faithful. I thank You for providing an opportunity for us to partner with You by aligning ourselves to Your will. So Lord I pray for the unmarried who may worry about what tomorrow holds. Help them cast their cares upon You. Help them trust in You. Remind them that You hold the future in Your hands and Your plans are perfect. Father, we have our wants and desires, but we ask that You align our hearts with Your will. Help us not to rely on our own understanding and our own strength but help us to rely on You alone. Amen.

Small Group Discussion 6

1. Do you actively pray for a relationship? How do you think God is currently responding to that prayer (yes, no or wait)?

2. Who is someone that you know is unmarried? Pray for them.

3. In what areas as an unmarried person do you need prayer? Pray and share this with others.

7

FUELED

I really want to use this chapter to speak directly to my brothers and sisters in Christ who deeply desire a relationship. The intention of this book, again, isn't to discourage you from pursuing a relationship. However, as believers, it's important that you do not allow your season of singleness to disrupt the way you pursue the Lord. Your relationship with the Lord is paramount and it will be the consistent thread from now to eternity. If you truly desire a relationship that glorifies God, then you must put Him first regardless of your relationship status. Having a strong relationship with God and strong godly values in your season of singleness is only going to help you, not hurt you as you journey towards pursuing a relationship.

Match, an online dating service, released its 12th annual "Singles In America" study in Nov. 2022. The study is said to be the largest and most comprehensive "annual study on single adults, as they surveyed over 5,000 single men and women. Although this is not a Christian specific study, it may still be helpful in understanding how unmarried Christians feel in their current season of life.

According to the study, 70% of all singles are open to finding a relationship (73% men and 66% women) and single adults in America are 48% more ready than ever to settle down and get married.[1] I would venture to believe those numbers aren't too different for believers. So if you greatly desire a relationship, this chapter is specifically written to encourage you in your pursuit.

In Chapter 5, I focused on the importance of being content in Christ. In this Chapter, I want to expound upon how your deep desire for marriage may not be discontentment but fuel. There may be some of you who feel like your lack of a relationship is simply unfair. There may be others that feel discouraged or may think that God has forgotten about them in this area. If that's you, I completely understand your pain and I sympathize with you.

Since 2020, I have felt more prepared for a relationship than I have ever been in my life. My desire hasn't been lustful or for selfish gain. Although, I absolutely have had to wrestle with those feelings. Make no mistake about it, I have definitely struggled with wanting a relationship simply because of lust and selfish gain. However, that has not primarily been the reason for my desire to be in a relationship, especially in recent years. As mentioned, I have absolutely had

---

[1] "Singles in America," *Match*, November 15, 2022, https://www.sin-glesinamerica.com/

moments of true discontent and it's a constant battle. But that's not the source of my desire to be married.

It's hard to explain, but for the past several years I've just had this growing desire to be used by God in the capacity of marriage. There is this yearning to have a marriage that can be viewed as not only *a* ministry, but my *first* ministry. I look forward to leading my bride and our family, to praying with them, to discipling them, and I actually, in a weird way, am excited for the low seasons that will inevitably come because I know that the Lord will equip us for them.

Let me be clear, I am whole without a relationship because I have the Lord. I also dedicate my life to serving God and others, fully, even without a relationship. However, I feel like there's a part of who I am that has yet to be used to the degree it would in marriage. I feel like there's a part of me that has been reserved for my bride and I'm eager to tap into it. So I think much of my desire to be married is that I really desire to have a kingdom relationship. I desire to have a relationship that truly glorifies God and benefits the kingdom. I am convinced that this desire is a gift from the Lord.

Therefore, I believe for the most part, my desire hasn't resulted in discontent but fuel. It has fueled me to continue developing my relationship with the Lord, because how can marriage be a ministry for me if I'm not being led by Him? It has fueled me to have standards, because why would I offer something so sacred to just anybody? It has also fueled me to continue working on improving myself so that I can enter a relationship as a healthy version of myself. Since I have a desire to get married, I would like to think that I have an awareness of how I act in my unmarried season could rollover into marriage.

Some of the primary reasons dating relationships fail are poor communication skills and lack of finances or financial stewardship. The cool thing about not yet being in a relationship, yet desiring one, is that you have an opportunity to address these common areas in which relationships fail.

Communication Skills

Communicating is something I feel that I'm good at as a person who is both a ministry leader and family leader. However, as I get older and have more experience leading people, I increasingly become more aware of my communication style and tendencies. I am very much a perfectionist and a reformer - not in a political sense, but I am a person who stands up for what is right or what I perceive to be right.

My communication style often reflects those characteristics. I often try to make sure I cover every base when it comes to either written or verbal communication. I want to prevent anyone from telling me that they misunderstood me or misinterpreted me. However, what I have discovered is that when someone *does* misunderstand or misinterpret me, I tend to take it personally. I tend to get hard on myself and think that I've made a mistake. Or even worse, I become resentful to the other person for not completely understanding what I've communicated.

I have learned that this is a result of me being a perfectionist. I don't like to make mistakes. When I don't make a mistake and yet I'm questioned, it frustrates me. It's like the person is saying I did something wrong or miscommunicated something. I'm growing in this area as I know that is not a healthy mindset to have. I also know that this could show itself greatly within a relationship. So it has been something that I've been working on outside of a relationship.

Poor communication skills within a relationship are often magnified when it comes to conflict resolution. Arguments are inevitable within relationships, but the question is, do you argue well? Before you enter into a dating relationship, pay close attention to how you argue. Are you a person who tends to initiate arguments? Are you a yeller? Are you more passive? This is another area in which I've paid close attention to my tendencies.

I am not one who typically initiates an argument, although I am not at all afraid to confront things, especially if I feel that I or someone else has been wronged. However, I'm not a complainer, for the most part, and I just am not often the person to start an argument. Yet, I have found that when an argument does start and I begin to feel disrespected, I begin to get into that "standing up for what I deem right" mode. It takes a lot for me to yell, but I can be triggered by what I deem disrespectful.

I haven't had many arguments with friends. I would say the bigger ones tend to be with family. One thing I have learned as I get older is that to argue well, you must first listen well. That isn't always reciprocated by the other individual, but you must become a better listener. I try to really listen and hear what the other person is saying because sometimes they are hurting about something that doesn't necessarily stem from me or something that I did. It may be something else that has triggered those emotions. I can't control how that person is acting, but I can control how I respond. So I've become more intentional about listening first. This is scriptural as well: "My dearly loved brothers, understand this: Everyone must be quick to hear, slow to speak, and slow to anger, for man's anger does not accomplish God's righteousness," (James 1:19-20).

Scripture isn't telling you not to speak. It also isn't telling you not to be angry. It says to be slow to speak and slow to anger. That certainly isn't the natural reaction for most people. I sometimes fail, but it's something I try to be intentional about while arguing.

In a relationship, it will be important for both individuals to serve each other well by being slow to speak and slow to anger. But again, you can't control the way another person acts. It's important for you to become intentional about developing these habits before entering into a relationship. You won't always do it right, but these are important traits to develop.

Another tendency I have when it comes to arguments is I typically get over things really quickly. I'm not one who holds grudges and stays mad. I've always thought this was a good trait and in some ways it is. However, a friend of mine who has been married over 10 years gave me some good advice in my mid-20s. He told me that in a relationship, just because you're over something doesn't necessarily mean the other person is. He told me that it will be important to still have good communication and make sure the other person has a chance to overcome as well. I thought that was solid advice and something that I have practiced even outside of a romantic relationship.

Finances

When it comes to a lack of finances or financial stewardship, I would say the latter is what's most important. Having a solid job and being financially stable is important. Our pursuit of money (or pursuit of someone with money) can oftentimes damage our pursuit of a godly relationship. I would say that financial stewardship is a major key. How do you steward your money? Are you spending it on every new sneaker drop? Are you spending it lavishly on clothes or electronics? Do you believe in living life with an open hand and willing to support those in need or your church? These are questions we must ask, definitely about others when we enter a relationship, but also about ourselves. You don't have to be in a relationship to answer these questions. Really, questions like these should be answered prior to a relationship. You should be practicing good financial habits even in your unmarried and non-dating season.

It was Jesus who said this in His famous Sermon On The Mount: "Don't collect for yourselves treasures on earth, where moth and rust destroy and where thieves break in and steal. But collect for yourselves treasures in heaven, where neither moth nor rust destroys, and where thieves don't break in and steal. For where your treasure is, there your heart will be also (Matthew 6:19-21)." We must understand that when Jesus commands us not to collect for treasures on earth, He's not merely talking about money. He's talking about anything we value most and above Him. For many, that is money. For others, it's job titles or prestige. Jesus is not telling us not to make money and not to have good jobs, He's saying not to cherish those things above all.

Some people are this way when it comes to relationships. You have some who want to make big money so that they can, in their mind, become more attractive. You have others who will only pursue a relationship if they know that person has money. Whether you have money or not isn't the issue and that's not what Jesus is getting at in scripture. How you steward your money and how you value it is what Jesus essentially says. In fact, He tells us that our heart will be reflected in the way we store our treasure. If you're living life with a closed hand and all you're doing is mounting possessions for yourself in this life, you are in error. You can learn a lot about a person's heart by just observing how that person stewards their finances. Now is the time, in your unmarried and non-dating season, to build healthy financial habits.

Delighting in the Lord

I can't stress enough how important it is for the unmarried person and those who are not actively dating to delight in the Lord. Psalms 37:4 says: "Take delight in the Lord, and He will give you your heart's desires." These words have often been misinterpreted and manipulated into a gospel message that says, "You can get whatever you want from the Lord if you delight in Him," and that's not what the verse is saying. I do not think that God is anti-pleasure or anti-joy. He's not a joy-snatcher.

I think what the Lord wants us to understand is that when we delight in Him, He becomes our ultimate joy. If we delight in the Lord, He is who we want most and He is faithful to give more of Himself to us. I know this can seem like another, "Well, your desires don't matter" sentiment to the unmarried believer, but I don't think that is what the Lord is saying. When you delight in the Lord, He fills and satisfies you and makes the hard waiting enjoyable.

I like what Proverbs 27:7 says: "A person who is full tramples on a honeycomb, but to a hungry person, any bitter thing is sweet." Pastor Josh Howerton says it this way, "When your appetite goes up, your standards go down. Never go grocery shopping when you're hungry. If you are not settled in your relationship with Christ, you'll settle for Mr. (or Mrs.) Right-Now, instead of waiting for Mr. or Mrs. Right."[2]

When you are not feasting upon the Bread of Life and drinking from the Fountain of Living Water, you are prone to starve and settle for whatever comes your way. This is tremendously important for the unmarried believer. When you are void of a relationship yet desire one, it can sometimes feel like you're starving for one. This can lead to, as scripture says, even bitter things becoming seemingly sweet. We must be careful.

This is why it's so important to delight in the Lord. Your desire for a relationship is absolutely *not* a bad thing, but don't lose sight of your relationship with the Lord. Delight in Him and He will fill you. Your desire for a relationship must be fueled by a love for God and in return, I believe He will fuel you in your pursuit of marriage.

---

[2] Howerton, Josh [josh_howerton]. "The Most Important Verse in the Bible about Dating." *Instagram*, April 18, 2023, https://www.instagram.com/p/CrLbw7luqGQ/?utm_source=ig_web_copy_link&igshid=MzRlODBiNWFlZA%3D%3D

Small Group Discussion 7

1. Do you feel that you are ready for a relationship right now? Why or why not?

2. Are there traits or areas of your life you'd like to improve upon before getting into a relationship?

3. Do you find it difficult to delight yourself in the Lord while unmarried? Why or why not?

8

The Gospel for All

One of the biggest misconceptions that people have of unmarried Christians is that they're at some sort of impasse in life. Some people may not say it blatantly, but it comes across this way—that you are limited to what you will be able to accomplish outside of wedlock. I've heard it indirectly said to me plenty of times. It's always something along the lines of, "I see you're walking in your calling, now all you need is a wife and you'll really be on your way." Whether it is meant this way or not, it can come across as needing a spouse to accomplish certain things in life.

My grandfather used to always tell me that it wasn't until he married my grandmother that his art career began to surge. But I don't think he was telling me that because I needed a wife to reach a certain level in life. I think he was just hammering a point that women can make you better. I completely agree with that notion. God created women to be helpers. It's in their DNA to help. My grandfather had been working for years at advancing his art career. He didn't intentionally seek a wife so that his art career would reach a new height. I think that's the distinction that must be made.

It reminds me of views that some have of the gospel that is not the gospel at all. I believe the gospel both saves and sends. Ephesians 2:8-9 says: "For you are saved by grace through faith, and this is not from yourselves; it is God's gift - not from works, so that no one can boast."

It is clear that we are not saved by our works. Salvation is a free gift that anyone can receive by grace through faith in Jesus. You don't have to work for it, you don't need to be married, you don't even need to clean yourself up prior to placing your faith in Jesus. The only requirement is that you believe. Therefore, the only thing that can disqualify you from this free gift is disbelief.

So the gospel saves. But the gospel also sends. The very next verse in Ephesians 2 says this: "For we are His creation, created in Christ Jesus for good works, which God prepared ahead of time so that we should walk in them."

It is not by works that we are saved, but after the gospel has saved you and lifted you from the pit, the gospel sends you to do good works. For we are His creation and our hearts have been regenerated by Christ Jesus. Therefore, He sends us to do good works. He sends us to reflect Him. He sends us to be His hands and feet. He has commissioned us to go make disciples of all nations, baptizing them in the name of the Father and of the Son and of the Holy Spirit, teaching them to observe everything He has commanded (Matthew 28:18-20).

This "sending" is not limited to a certain group of believers, it is given to *all* believers. It doesn't matter if you are married or unmarried. It doesn't even matter if you never get married. The gospel is sending you out into a broken world that so desperately needs to hear it and nothing should stand in the way of that.

We create requirements that the Lord never created. We draw lines that the Lord never drew. Jesus saves all who come to Him in faith and He sends all who believe in Him to do a mighty work for the kingdom. Therefore, you do not have to be married to walk in the calling God has placed on your life. Yet, many carry this belief that essentially you have not graduated as a Christian if you are not married. It's as if you must be stuck in some elementary form of Christianity until you marry. This is simply not the case.

Unmarried Biblical Characters

We see several examples of God using unmarried people in the bible to do an amazing work for the kingdom of God. The following are just a few:

Jeremiah is an example of an unmarried person in the bible who was called for a great work. In fact, the Lord forbade Jeremiah from getting married. The book of Jeremiah chapter 16 has an entire section, verses 1-16 that is titled, "No Marriage for Jeremiah." It's actually a little funny when you first read that title. But the Lord commanded Jeremiah not to marry for a reason.

It says this in Jeremiah 16:1-4, "The word of the Lord came to me: "You must not marry or have sons or daughters in this place. For this is what the Lord says concerning sons and daughters born in this place as well as concerning the mothers who bear them and the fathers who father them in this land: They will die from deadly diseases. They will not be mourned or buried but will be like manure on the face of the earth. They will be finished off by sword and famine. Their corpses will become food for the birds of the sky and for the wild animals of the land." God wanted to protect Jeremiah from anguish. Jeremiah would have lost his family to diseases if He stepped outside the will of God. So Jeremiah went on to live a productive life for the Lord as an unmarried man.

There's also Ruth, who yes, ended up marrying. But much of what we see in her story is her not being married. God used Ruth in her unmarried state to display tremendous sacrificial love and faith toward God and Naomi.

There's also Joseph of the Old Testament. Much like Ruth, Joseph would eventually marry. But much of his story is spent as an unmarried man. God used him greatly during that season of his life and Joseph exuded tremendous obedience to the Lord. Joseph demonstrated purity and self-control when Potiphar's wife attempted to sleep with him. Joseph was then thrown into prison as an innocent man, but he continued to grow in his affection for the Lord. Scripture even says that because the Lord was with Joseph, He made everything he did successful.

John the Baptist is another example of an unmarried man who did great work for the kingdom of God. This man baptized many people, including Jesus the Savior of the world! Surely being unmarried did not prevent the Lord from using him.

Then there's the Apostle Paul who lived fervently for the Lord. Paul wrote most of the New Testament. He did this as an unmarried man.

As a person who is entering into pastoral ministry, I'll be honest that I feel the heat cranking up. I feel the pressure to get married becoming more and more prevalent. There's this belief that pastors must be married and if they are not, that's a big red flag. They may doubt that an unmarried pastor will be able to speak into the lives of families without their own spouse and kids. They may also just simply view the unmarried pastor as weird or respect the pastor less because they have no spouse.

But wisdom is not merely gained through experiences and experiences are not more valuable than the Word of God. An unmarried Pastor who stands on the truth of Scripture has much to say about families. A Pastor being unmarried should not make you uncomfortable. It can actually be a beautiful thing. Sure there may be some pastors who are unmarried because they lack the ability to commit, but I'm certain the overwhelming majority of pastors that are unmarried are not afraid of commitment. In fact, quite the contrary, they are extremely committed to God and His people.

Pastors are not the only ones treated this way by the Church. This kind of treatment is evident in the lives of many unmarried Christians, whether they are in vocational ministry or not. They too can be faced with pressure to marry so that they can advance as believers and even their careers in the marketplace.

God is working in the lives of every believer regardless of their economic status, ethnicity and even their marital status. It is absolutely true that having a spouse can benefit you in ministry or in the marketplace, but I always lean on this hard truth: God will do what is best for His glory and the good of His people. Therefore, that can mean what's best for God's glory and the good of His people is you being unmarried. There is great work that can flow from that status. Likewise, it can mean what's best for God's glory and the good of His people is you being married. There is definitely great kingdom work that can come from that status. God will provide for the plans He has for your life. We must trust Him.

There's also an aspect to this that is super important for us to remember. Both the married and unmarried carry a beautiful opportunity to reflect elements of the gospel. For the married couple, their love should mirror Christ's sacrificial love for the Church. Also, the submissive love the Church has for Christ should be reflected in a married person's submission to their spouse (Ephesians 5). For the unmarried person, there is a wonderful opportunity to reflect a Christian's ultimate identity in Christ.

In 1 Corinthians 6:17, we read, "'But anyone joined to the Lord is one spirit with Him.'" As unmarried people, we are not and should not be joined into one flesh with the opposite sex outside of marriage. So then, who are the unmarried joined to when their life is devoted unto the Lord? Scripture says we are joined to the Lord! Isn't that a beautiful thing?

Therefore, the unmarried person who is joined to the Lord is complete. They have all they need to complete whatever the Lord has set before them, regardless of their marital status. A spouse does not complete you. Sex does not complete you. Everything you could ever need is found in our precious Lord and Savior, Jesus.

The unmarried person, just like married people, reflects the believer's eternal identity with the Church. Worldly culture suggests that a person who is not married is a person who is alone and lonely. However, married or unmarried, those who are in Christ are never alone. Although a believer may not be married, they are still a believer and because of this there is a church body who surrounds them and loves them. Genesis 2:18 tells us that it is not good for man to be alone and this indeed is true. Thank God for His saving grace and that we are able to step into a family as children of God—an eternal family. It is because of this that we believers, even the unmarried, never have to worry about being alone.

I spent my early 20s extremely focused on advancing my journalism career. The Lord blessed me with an opportunity to become a credentialed media member covering Washington's NFL Team now known as the Commanders. It's an achievement I'm proud of as it's uncommon for young journalists to gain the access I had. It's even more uncommon for black journalists. While the opportunity to cover a sport I love was awesome, I quickly realized how the Lord was using that platform to minister. I had two separate occasions where a fan of the team who followed my work reached out to me with questions about the Gospel. Those conversations, and I'm certain other people God placed in their lives, helped lead them to faith in Jesus. So even as a young man who was not only unmarried, but not pursuing marriage at that point, God was working in my life.

I also spent those years of my life developing as a worship leader and minister. I would spend countless hours in my basement discovering my sound and writing worship music. Those songwriting sessions always pushed me closer to Scripture, which in turn pushed me closer to God. That time spent with God became an overflow in the way I ministered. Even now as an unmarried 30-year old who desires to be married, I am not allowing my unmarried status to stop me from moving in the call God has on my life.

We must not consider our relationship status a requirement to do kingdom work. As long as there is breath in our lungs, the Gospel is sending us. God is able to use all believers to reflect His goodness. He does this all for His glory and the good of His people.

Small Group Discussion 8

1. Reflect on how God has used you even while unmarried. Do you see evidence of Him using your relationship status for His glory and the good of others?

2. Does it ever feel like people view you as incapable of fully walking in your calling without a spouse? How do you deal with that?

3. Are you using your unmarried status to reflect elements of the gospel?

9

The Great Wedding Ceremony

This may be difficult for us to grasp. It may be too vast for us to understand, but there will come a day when every believer will wed. While there is no guarantee that a believer will get married in this life, God promises a day when every believer will enter an eternal union with Christ.

Revelation 19:6-9 says this, "Then I heard something like the voice of a vast multitude, like the sound of cascading waters, and like the rumbling of loud thunder, saying: Hallelujah, because our Lord God, the Almighty, has begun to reign! Let us be glad, rejoice, and give Him glory, because the marriage of the Lamb has come, and His wife has prepared herself. She was given fine linen to wear, bright and pure. For the fine linen represents the righteous acts of the saints. Then he said to me, 'Write: Those invited to the marriage feast of the Lamb are fortunate!' He also said to me,

'These words of God are true.'" What a day this will be! Not even the greatest pleasures this world has to offer can compare. Jesus will return soon and He's returning for His bride! Are you preparing yourself?

It is interesting that this passage says the Lord's wife (the Church) "prepared herself." It says that the Church was "given fine linen to wear, bright and pure. For the linen represents the righteous acts of the saints."

In biblical times, though this varied throughout history, there was a betrothal period in which the bride and groom were separated until marriage. During this time, the bride would prepare herself for marriage. It was a time for her to adjust to her new family and ready her belongings. Similarly, the Church must prepare herself for her bridegroom. We must prepare ourselves during this period. Scripture says that the fine linen we've been given represents the righteous acts of the saints. Therefore, those who have been saved by Christ have become the bride of Christ and have been sent to do righteous acts until the day they enter eternal union with Christ. The Lord does not make marriage in this life a requirement for these righteous acts to be done. Whether you marry or not in this life, you will be married someday when our Lord returns. We may not know the day nor the hour, but "these words of God are true" (Revelation 22:6). The Lord will return for His bride and He's returning for a bride that is bright and pure. He is returning for a bride that has prepared herself with righteous acts.

Scripture tells us that faith without works is dead (James 2:20). Works do not save us, for it is by grace through faith that we are saved. However, when you have been saved, faith should be active together with works. For by works, our faith is perfected (James 2:22). I believe James 4:17 makes it super clear, "So it is a sin for the person who knows to do what is good and doesn't do it." If we have Jesus, we have knowledge of what is good. Through God's holy Word and through the Holy Spirit, we are led to know what is right.

The unmarried must not forsake this truth. Do not waste the gift of being unmarried. The Lord has a major work for you to do right here and now. Your ultimate goal in life should be to love God and to love all people. You should desire to do what's best for God's glory and the good of His people. The Holy Spirit will equip you for this task.

Trust me, I understand how difficult it can be for the person who desires marriage. Every single day I am tempted to focus on the idea of marriage and who I might marry. While there is nothing wrong with considering these things, again, we can become so engulfed by the idea of marriage that it becomes an idol. I struggle with this.

I often have to remind myself to focus most on Christ. Matthew 22:37-38 commands us to "Love the Lord your God with all your heart, with all your soul, and with all your mind. This is the greatest and most important command." When we idolize things, ideas or people, we are in fact not loving the Lord with all our heart, all our soul and all our mind. This goes against what the Lord has commanded us. He does not want half our hearts, half our souls and half our minds; He wants all of us. The Lord desires everything and He is worthy of everything we have and are.

For those living a life committed to never marrying as a way to glorify the Lord, it can be equally difficult. God loves you and has great plans for you. He will strengthen you and bring peace. Truly glorify the Lord with your gift of being unmarried.

The Lord has also called us to love others. We are to love our neighbor as ourselves (Matthew 22:39). Therefore, we remind ourselves of who we are in Christ. We are loved, we are forgiven, we have everything we need and we are free from the bondage of sin. This knowledge of who we are in Christ should not merely be for ourselves, it should cause us to love others well. For we know that had it not been for Christ, we would be dead in sin. We have not saved ourselves. We also know that it is the Lord who sustains us. We literally have nothing to boast about but Jesus! (Ephesians 2:8-9).

God will do what is best for His glory and the good of His people. If you experience marriage in this life, praise the Lord! If not, praise the Lord! There will be a day better than any day any person married or unmarried will ever experience. There will be a day when we no longer have to face earthly temptations. There will be a day where we will experience no more pain and no more sadness. Lift your head to the Savior of the world, for He is coming soon! But until that day comes, there is great work to be done. Let us prepare for the coming of our Savior.

Revelation 21:1-6 – *"Then I saw a new heaven and a new earth, for the first heaven and the first earth had passed away, and the sea no longer existed. I also saw the Holy City, new Jerusalem, coming down* *out of heaven from God, prepared like a bride adorned for her husband. Then I heard a loud voice from the throne: Look! God's dwelling is with humanity, and He will live with them. They will be His people, and God Himself will be with them and be their God. He will wipe away every tear from their eyes. Death will no longer exist; grief, crying, and pain will exist no longer, because the previous things have passed away. Then the One seated on the throne said, 'Look! I am making everything new.' He also said, 'Write, because these words are faithful and true.' And He said to me, 'It is done! I am the Alpha and the Omega, the Beginning and the End. I will give water as a gift to the thirsty from the spring of life.'"*

Come, Lord Jesus, come!

Small Group Discussion 9

1. How does it make you feel to know that you, as a believer, are the bride of Christ?

2. Are you preparing yourself for the second coming of our Lord and Savior?

3. Do you struggle with making marriage an Idol? How do you combat that?

About the Author

Emmanual Benton is a pastor, singer/songwriter, and entrepreneur from Fort Washington, MD. He is a former credentialed journalist that covered Washington's NFL team. His work garnered features and recognition from the Washington Post and ESPN, among other major outlets. In 2018, Emmanual accepted God's call into ministry. Since then, he has released three worship songs, including his latest "Your Love Endures Forever," and he currently serves as one of the pastors at Avert Church in Waldorf, MD.

www.ingramcontent.com/pod-product-compliance
Lightning Source LLC
Chambersburg PA
CBHW041210150726
48006CB00016B/2187